Libya and Change: How It Happened

Thomas L. Hodge, M.A.

Libya and Change

With the struggles that have recently been going on in the Middle East, one would begin to wander what has sociologically occurred in the area to affect such change. "Marx commitment to social change led him to visualize social systems as rife with change-producing conflict." (Turner, 1975) The instances of revolution in Libya, Egypt, Sudan, Yemen, and several other countries are prime examples of Marx's idea of conflict producing change. This can easily be seen when looking at each of the countries that have been undergoing revolution over the past year. Conflict theory can typically be noticed and well understood as an explanation of such changes during the pivotal moments of political change. It can clearly be noted by the public that there are oppressed individuals when the masses revolt against the ruling authorities. The conditions can be clearly seen in each country that lead up to the revolts.

The Libya is a prime example to examine concerning the revolt against and overthrowing of the ruling class. The westernized countries of the world have known for quite some time about the issues with the ruling class of Libya. This ruling class has been figurehead by Muammar Gaddafi since January of 1970. Interestingly, Gaddafi came to power in Libya as part of coup d'état that had begun in September of 1969. The reason for the coup was to make changes to the political system of Libya as a consensus of the people felt that Sansui Dynasty and the ruling King Muhammad Idrīs was out of place and anachronistic. The coup can also be seen as a response to the drastic class differences between the ruling class of the country and middle and lower classes of Libya. The coup involved no bloodshed and was incredibly quick in its execution. King Idris was detained the military officers that headed the coup for a week. After his week being held in prison, he announced to the people that he would resign his throne.

Immediately after the coup, the Revolutionary Command Council was formed by the twelve military officers that were responsible for heading the movement to overthrow the prior monarchy. The Revolutionary Command Council reorganized and restructured itself during the four month period following the coup. Finally, the council decided to choose from among its members a spokesperson. They chose to promote Captain Muammar Gaddafi to the rank of Colonel and make him their spokesperson to the public. In an interested twist, they also decided that he should be the commander-in-chief of the Libyan Army at the same time. This move by the council, in turn, made Gaddafi the head of state for Libya.

In view of the history of the 1969 coup in Libya, one can compare and contrast clearly the similarities and differences between the 1969 coup and the rebellion of 2011 in Libya. In 2011, Gaddafi was still in power as the de-facto ruler of Libya. He developed his own ideas about how to run his country. "Nevertheless, in the early 1970s he set out to prove himself a leading political philosopher, developing something called the third universal theory, outlined in his famous Green Book." (Asser, 2011) Some lessons were learned by Gaddafi since he was a part of the original coup that brought him to power. He kept his military weak and ensured that political positions were filled by his supporters in order to decrease opposition to his rule of Libya. Gaddafi looked politics from the perspective of a military strategist who made decisions based on the purpose of controlling his people and countering his opposing forces. "The model that was created in reality was an ultra-hierarchical pyramid - with the Gaddafi family and close allies at the top wielding power unchecked, protected by a brutal security apparatus." (Asser, 2011)

The revolt, however, began as a reaction to Gaddafi's attempts at controlling opposition before the outbreak of open rebellion would occur. The revolution began as a protest to housing issues in Libya. Libyan police arrested several leaders of the protest on controversial charges. This fueled the flames of revolution in Libya. The beginnings of the revolt in Libya can be seen as reminiscent of the demonstration held at Kent State University in May of 1970. The protests were peaceful in the beginning. The purpose was not to overthrow the government but for change to the existing structure for the betterment of the society. However, the immediate reactions to the protests in Libya were drastically different from the protest at Kent State. Gaddafi saw that if he was to try to correct the official for their acts upon the people. It could be seen as a weakness. In the prior coup, the weaknesses of the ruling monarchy were the object of exploitation by the military coup. Gaddafi based the majority of his political strategy on not repeating the mistakes that King Idris made in 1969.

Over the past several months since February 2011, the revolt has pushed its way across Libya for the purpose removing the existing powers of Gaddafi from rule. The change has brought much bloodshed to the country as Gaddafi has struggled to maintain control of the country and his weakened military. The tightened grip of Gaddafi's control had caused many of his military leaders to defect. Some defected to the rebel forces, and some defected to other countries because they did not wish to follow what they had seen as unlawful orders to harm the people of Libya. The revolt has so far been successful in gaining some control of the country, and the revolutionaries currently have put into place a National Transitional Council as the official representative body for Libya.

The overthrow of 2011 was much different than that of 1969. While the 1969 incident was a military coup that was conspired by a small group, the 2011 coup was the actions of numerous individuals who were reacting to the pressures that the ruling group had imposed on them. The '69 coup leaders reasoned their purpose as being that the ruling class was not deserving of their power because the king was anachronistic. In 2011, the revolutionaries had a different claim. They did not feel so much that the ruling was not deserving of their power, but that such power had been abused and was no longer beneficial to the people as a whole. Also, it can clearly be seen that the ruling monarchy in 1969 did not struggle against the change as Gaddafi's regime had struggled against its opposition.

While examining the two revolutions, there are numerous theories to be considered in addressing the happenings. A primary concept to note when looking at revolutions is the concept of reactance. Burke, Lake, and Paine explained, "This hypothetical motivational state is in response to the reduction (or threatened reduction) of one's potential for acting, and conceptually may be considered a counter force" (2009). Reactance is a very important concept when examining the response from a perspective of sociological conflict theory. The conflict among the ruling class that is in power against the working class creates a conflict and a struggle for resources among the people due to scarcity. The class that is in power will attempt to limit the lower class or working class for the purpose of hoarding those resources. These resources can be tangible or non-tangible resource.

Power itself could be a potential resource. "Power-the ability to influence the outcomes of other people-is a key variable that regulates a wide range of human social interactions." (Maner, Kaschak, & Jones, 2010) The ruling class (as in the case of Gaddafi) might feel the need to protect their power because it is a limited resource. To protect that power from having to be disbursed to others, Gaddafi threatened the freedoms of the working class and regular people of his country. In doing so, Gaddafi failed to take into consideration the theory of reactance. The recent social movement in Libya that has led to a state of revolution is a clear indication of the people as a whole reacting to the oppression of the ruling class (the Gaddafi regime). The coup in 1969 can be explained by conflict theory through reactance as can be seen as the military group felt that they should assume the power from the ruling monarchy. The 1969 incident shows how power is the object of the coup. The military factions overthrew the existing monarchy in order to assume the power for themselves.

The strain theory can also be seen an explanation of the events in the incidents in Libya also. The strain theory is a theory that addresses criminal behavior typically. "The motivation to deviance adduced by the strain theorist is so strong that we can well understand the deviant act even assuming the deviant believes it is wrong." (Clarke & Kelly, 2008) In strain theory, criminals are pressured to commit crimes due to the forces exerted on them by the society to achieve certain goals. Based on what were viewed as social norms in the Libyan society, the rebel forces were under pressures to be successful with the resources that were available to them. Unfortunately, the restraints that were placed on them by Gaddafi's regime placed abnormally high levels of pressure and stress on the individuals. This pressure provided them with the choice of responding in an innovative, ritualistic, retreatist, or rebellious way. The goal would have been to live a prosperous life as the Libyans had lived since the regime had taken over. If they would have been innovative, they would have just found new ways to do achieve this goal. If they would have responded ritualistically, they would have just been accepting the means that had been given them, but they would have had to give up on the goal of being prosperous. The retreatist would have tried more to set themselves off from the society. The Libyans instead chose to rebel against the standing system. They chose to change the means and the goals and the system as a whole.

When looking at the recent revolution in Libya, one could look at the event as if the rebellion was a norm. The idea that rebellion is a deviant act that goes against the social norm would almost seem like a simple straight forward answer, but it depends on the perspective from which the rebellion is examined. In the context of the history of human societies, the Libyan revolution could be viewed as a norm. Throughout history, groups of oppressed people have opted to rebel against the standing authority on numerous occasions. Some of the examples include the formation of the United States, France on numerous occasions during the eighteenth and nineteenth centuries, the Russian revolution in the early twentieth century, and any other country that has had a dramatic and rapid restructuring of their norms by force. Throughout history, there have been numerous cases in which oppressed groups have rose up in revolution against the ruling parties. With this in mind, it can be said that rebellion is the norm for certain types of oppression throughout history.

Depending on the sociological viewpoint that one takes, the Libyan revolution can take many differing forms and be explained a variety of different ways. From the functionalist view of the incident, one can easily see that the rebellion was the result of stresses placed upon the rebellious group that was caused by divisions among the classes of people in the country. The social inequalities resulted in an overthrowing of the existing structure and implementation of a new structure. If the gap between the Libyan social classes drifts again, the inequalities could causes pressures again upon the classes that could result in the restructuring of the social system of the country yet again.

One of the primary errors that Gaddafi made while in power was to dismiss the class struggles of his own people. Instead, he put further pressure on the lower classes which resulted in the rebellion. When he put pressures on his senior military officials, they reacted by defecting from his regime due to the pressures that were put on them to destroy the rebellion. When a ruling class disregards the needs of the working class, the elite class incites those people to reactance and defiance against those who are in charge.

The Libyan revolution can also be seen as an example of latent function also. Peraino (2008) examined the fact that Libyan town of Darnah accounted for a significantly high number of anti-American insurgents during

Operation Iraqi Freedom. The small town of Darnah was one of the first towns that were involved in the protests that began the uprising in Libya. The training that several of the recruits gained during their exploits against the American forces in Iraq would later become useful during the uprising and revolution against Gaddafi's forces. Gaddafi made statements displaying how he was aware of the indirect effect of the involvement of numerous Libyans in the insurgents of Iraq. "Gaddafi claimed that the protesters were young people who had been manipulated by Osama bin Laden, al-Qaeda's leader, and were acting under the influence of hallucinogenic drugs." (Al Jazeera, 2011). It could be easy to think that Gaddafi was delusional with such a claim, but looking at the facts, he may have had a point on at least part of his statement. Some of the revolutionaries could have been influenced by the teaching of the Islamic fundamentalist like Osama bin Laden and his followers. Many of the transient warriors that travel from Libya to places like Iraq and Afghanistan gained critical training from recruiters and Islamic radicals in combat tactics, guerrilla warfare, and terrorist operations. Upon returning to Libya, these young men directed their new-found abilities toward their homeland issues in Libya.

Looking deeper in Libya's history, one begins to see a cycle. This cycle has been continually repeating itself for centuries. "History always involves a dialectic relationship between thesis and antithesis, benevolence and perversion, leading to synthesis and renewal." (Floyd, 2007). History tends to repeat itself over and over. The cycle that Libya has fallen into is a cycle of violence, war, and restructuring of itself. During the twentieth century, the land that is now Libya has shifted from the Ottoman

Empire to the Italians to King Idris to Gaddafi. During and shortly after each shift, the new ruling authority promised improvements in the quality of life. Each group failed to deliver on that promise and only led the country into more turmoil, poverty, and chaos. This cycle has become a historical social norm for the country. This is one of several social norms for the country that has had a latent effect leading up to the most recent revolt in that has turned the country upside down again.

As human beings, people attempt to beat out history's cycles by taking steps to prevent the cycle from repeating. Certain human flaws always tend to get in the way, and history repeats itself eventually. Gaddafi is no exception to history repeating itself. Gaddafi's weaknesses included his hatred for the Westernized countries of the world, his paranoia of revolt from within his own ranks, and his evident cruelty to the people of his country. These are three facets that will be explored in more depth to demonstrate the application of several sociological theories that can be applied to the revolutions in Libya, the events that led up to the events, and several contributory events.

Gaddafi's dislike of European countries and America has been well-noticed by the West during the passing decades of his regime's rule. The westernized countries of the world had logical concerns about Gaddafi's involvement in the Pan Am flight 103 incident and numerous other incidents of state-sponsored terrorism. The state refused to extradite individuals that were involved in the Pan Am flight 103 bombing for a decade before eventually handing them over to the United Nation after numerous sanctions. (Washington Post, 1999). Gaddafi publicly made statements supporting extremist groups in radical Palestinian groups and Islamic terrorists in countries like Algeria and Tunisia. The UN has imposed numerous sanctions on the country throughout the years due to involvement in state-sponsored terrorism. This type of behavior from the ruling class that resulted in sanctions being imposed on the country of Libya from western countries planted seeds of hatred in the common people of Libya against the West. Later, this hatred can be seen as something that fueled individuals to join extremist groups for insurgent activities in Iraq.

Misdirecting the anger of the people would only last for so long. Eventually, the common people learn the truth about their circumstances. People start to question things over time. This is something that Gaddafi realized. Gaddafi was the leading benefactor from the 1969 coup. Because of his involvement in the previous revolt, Gaddafi knew what mistakes the previous ruling class made. This knowledge made Gaddafi paranoid. The paranoia led Gaddafi to weaken the military forces in Libya to where he could more easily control them. He appointed senior leadership that he felt he could trust. Uneducated masses are easier to control because they do not realize they are being controlled sometimes. If one is in charge, one can control the lower classes by several means. The lower classes can be segregated, separated, and turned against each other. This weakens the lower classes. One can also deprive the lower classes of the means by which they can improve themselves. One can reduce the numbers of individuals that oppose the ruling class. Many of these tactics were utilized by Gaddafi. A prime example would Gaddafi's personal guards. They were all women. This can easily be seen as an attempt to ensure that the closed security forces to him would be more easily control. In a Muslim culture, women are trained and ingrained to be submissive. It can be seen that Gaddafi's intentions were clear by the way that he utilized women as his personal guards because they would be seen as more easily controlled by Gaddafi in the Muslim culture. By being more submissive, they would be less likely to revolt against him to seize power like he had once done. This trend can be seen with much of his military forces in that they were ill-prepared, underfeed, under-supplied, and under-trained at the time of the revolt. It seems that there was a failure for Colonel Gaddafi to realize that this kind of treatment would have such a drastic effect on their moral and loyalty which would later to explain why so many of the pro-Gaddafi forces were so willing to quickly change sides in mid-conflict. The fact that the Libyan military was weakened due to Gaddafi's restraints can also be seen as a way in which ties to the existing regime were weakened also. If there are fewer individuals that are tightly connected to an organization (such as the Libyan government or military), there will be fewer common people that can relate to that organization. This would be contributory to the negative public opinion of the Gaddafi regime by the common people indirectly by reducing the number of positive connections to such an organization through ties to friends and family members of supportive service-members of the Libyan armed forces.

The issues with human rights violations in Libya have been well documented throughout the past several decades. "The government's human rights record remained poor. Citizens did not have the right to change their government. Continuing problems included reported disappearances; torture; arbitrary arrest; lengthy pretrial and sometimes incommunicado detention; official impunity; and poor prison conditions." (US

State Department, 2010). Due to the mistreatment of the common people of Libya and deprivation of the rights of the individuals, it is easy to understand how that numerous sociological theories can be so easily applied to the situation in the country leading up to and continuing through the revolution. This type of treatment of the people of Libya puts great strain on the people which causes more crime as can be explained by Strain Theory. The increased number of people deviating from what the elite classes seems to be a sociological norm that led to several subcultures that grow and feed themselves overtime. This is an example of subculture theory and also differential association theory. In times of great depression and hopelessness, people will rebel against the situation which pushed so far. In turn, this causes a phenomenon in which defying the norms that have been set in place by the ruling class become more normal than abnormal. This is an example of a culture reaching a state of anomie and also an example of phenomenological theory. The connection to phenomenological theory exists due to sensation that can be linked to individuals having an urge to defy the status quo. Finally, the class struggle between the wealthy and powerful elites of the society clash against the working class or impoverish lower class of the society in the all-out revolution that has served as the pivotal moment in history that has overturned the rule of Colonel Muammar Gaddafi.

The connections between theories can be seen in several events in Libyan history. The connection between the theories and overlapping application of the theories are exemplar of a grand and flowing design of sociological theory that is ever-changing. While looking deeper into the conflict, one can see the possibility for more theories to develop as a result of the revolution. Numerous references have been made about the use of technology has been made with direct reference to the events that have unfolded in the northern African country. Many people have alluded to a theory that the changes in nearby countries have spread throughout the region to have an effect on Libya contributing to the revolutionary movements that brought about the violent and forceful changes. Perhaps, there is more to the incident than just contributory spreading of ideas through use of the internet. By merging several theories together, one can notice that changes and conflict are a natural part of a society. If the pressures are imposed upon the society to attempt to contain these conflicts, frustrations arise. If the frustrations are oppressed and further amplified by controlling authorities, they will be redirected in some form. In Libya, the forces were often redirected toward Islamic extremist activities.

Eventually, the latent frustrations and pressures will arise and be redirected until changes occur within the existing systems to allow for the proper degree of conflict to come to equilibrium to allow the society to properly function. Therefore, conflict is purely functional for a society whether it is steady and controlled or it is volatile and intermittent. The latent conflicts within a society will become manifest and bring about sweeping changes to the existing norms of a society once a state of overwhelming pressure has been reached.

In conclusion, the plight of people of Libya serves as an interesting sociological study for theorists. Several theories can be applied to the coup of 1969 and the rebellion of 2011. The exploration of the occurrences should be further investigated to allow for a better understanding of how the unique cultural lessons that can be learned should be applied to better societies and address changes that occur throughout different parts of the world. Numerous existing social theories can be seen throughout the history of the country and the two major societal changes that have affected the country in 1969 and 2011. The events surrounding the Libyan revolution serve as a web of interconnected latencies that provided numerous contributory factors that provide the society with more energy pushing it into the revolt. There did not need to be one single catalytic event spark the beginning of the conflict. Change rarely occurs in one explosive and unexpected event. There are numerous signs of the oncoming change. Learning to define and describe these signs for the purpose of prediction and possible prevention would be very useful information for a ruling class. The change has now taken place in Libya yet again. Now the world will wait to see if the historical cycle of the Libyan people will repeat itself another time. Defining the history and trends of the Libyan society is very easily accomplished through observation and analysis of the historical events. The reasoning behind why the events occurred can easily be understood also. Social theories attempts to predict what the future will hold for countries like Libya, but only time will tell if these theories will be accurate.

References

Al Jazeera. (2011, February 25). Gaddafi blames Al-Queda for revolt. Retreived from http://english.aljazeera.net/news/africa/2011/02/20112254231296453.html

Asser, M. (2011). The Muammar Gaddafi story. Retreived from http://www.bbc.co.uk/news/world-africa-12688033

Burke, W. W., Lake, D. G., & Paine, J. W. (2009). Organization change: A comprehensive reader. San Francisco: Jossey-Bass.

Clarke, E. & Kelly, D. (2008). *Deviant Behavior*. New York, NY. Worth Publishers.

Engels, F. & Marx, K. (1888). *The Communist Manifesto*, Project Gutenberg. Retrieved from http://www.temoa.info/node/10722

Floyd, J. (2005). Visions for Global Justice through the Lens of Sarkar's Social Cycle. *Journal of Futures Studies.* 9(*3*), 47-60

Kicillof, A., & Starosta, G. (2007). Value form and class struggle: A critique of the autonomist theory of value. *Capital & Class*, 31(92), 13-40. Retrieved from EBSCO*host*.

Maner, J. K., Kaschak, M. P., & Jones, J. L. (2010). Social power and the advent of action. *Social Cognition*, 28(1), 122-132. Retrieved from EBSCO*host*.

Peraino, K. (2008, April 28). Destination Martyrdom. *Newsweek*. 24-30.

The Communist Manifesto. (2011). *Encyclopedia Britannica*. Retrieved from http://www.britannica.com/EBchecked/topic/129206/The-Communist-Manifesto

Turner, J. H. (1975). Marx and Simmel Revisited: Reassessing the Foundations of Conflict Theory. *Social Forces*, 53(4), 618-627. Retrieved from EBSCO*host*.

U.S. State Department. (2010). *2009 Human Rights Report: Libya*. Washington DC: US Government Printing Office.

Washington Post. (1999). The Bombing of Pan Am Flight 103 Time Line. Retrieved from http://www.washingtonpost.com/wp-srv/inatl/longterm/panam103/timeline.htm.